What Else Can I P' ...

CW00459073

Clarinet
Grade One

© International Music Publications Ltd
First published in 1996 by International Music Publications Ltd
International Music Publications Ltd is a Faber Music company
Bloomsbury House 74–77 Great Russell Street London WC1B 3DA
Series Editor: Mark Mumford
Cover designed by Lydia Merrills-Ashcroft
Music arranged and processed by Barnes Music Engraving Ltd
Printed in England by Caligraving Ltd
All rights reserved

ISBN10: 0-571-53055-9
EAN13: 978-0-571-53055-7

To buy Faber Music publications or to find out about the full range of titles available,
please contact your local music retailer or Faber Music sales enquiries:

Faber Music Ltd, Burnt Mill, Elizabeth Way, Harlow, CM20 2HX England
Tel: +44(0)1279 82 89 82   Fax: +44(0)1279 82 89 83
sales@fabermusic.com   fabermusic.com

Introduction

In this *What Else Can I Play?* collection you'll find sixteen popular tunes that are both challenging and entertaining.

The pieces have been carefully selected and arranged to create ideal supplementary material for young clarinettists who are either working towards or have recently taken a Grade One clarinet examination.

As the student progresses through the volume, technical demands increase and new concepts are introduced which reflect the requirements of the major Examination Boards. Suggestions and guidelines on breathing, dynamics and tempo are given for each piece, together with technical tips and performance notes.

Pupils will experience a wide variety of music, ranging from folk and classical through to showtunes and popular songs, leading to a greater awareness of musical styles.

Whether it's for light relief from examination preparation, or to reinforce the understanding of new concepts, this collection will enthuse and encourage all young clarinet players.

All through the night

Traditional

I've got no strings

Words by Ned Washington, Music by Leigh Harline

The British Grenadiers

Traditional

Scarborough fair

Traditional

Three little fishies
(Itty bitty poo)

Words and Music by Saxie Dowell

Country gardens

Traditional

Puff the magic dragon

Words and Music by Peter Yarrow and Leonard Lipton

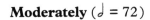

Moderately (♩ = 72)

8va

Mary's boy child

Words and Music by Jester Hairston

Smoothly (♩ = 108)

Clarinet

Piano

Bye bye blackbird

Words by Mort Dixon, Music by Ray Henderson

Francis Day & Hunter Ltd, London WC2H 0EA and Redwood Music Ltd, London NW1 8BD

Don't bring Lulu

Words by Billy Rose and Lew Brown, Music by Ray Henderson

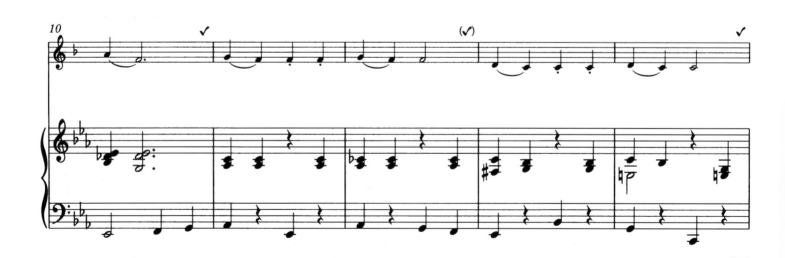

I'm forever blowing bubbles

Words and Music by Jaan Kenbrovin and John William Kellette

Oh, what a beautiful mornin'

Words by Oscar Hammerstein II, Music by Richard Rodgers

Who's afraid of the big bad wolf?

Words and Music by Frank Churchill. Additional lyrics by Ann Ronell

Flash, bang, wallop!

Words and Music by David Heneker

Minuet

J. S. Bach

I'm Popeye the sailor man

Words and Music by Sammy Lerner

Welcome to …

Paul Harris's
Clarinet Basics

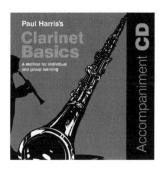

Clarinet Basics is a landmark method by one of the leading figures in clarinet education. It starts at absolute beginner level and progresses to about Grade 2 level. The method is set out in 22 stages, each of which includes:

- a wonderful variety of concert pieces from the great composers

- traditional tunes and fun, original exercises

- 'finger gyms' and 'warm ups' to help establish a sound technique

- invaluable 'fact files' and 'quizzes' to teach notation and general musicianship

- helpful, clear 'fingering charts' and 'rhythm boxes'

- great illustrations!

The separate teacher's book contains clarinet and piano accompaniments, suggestions for group work and teaching tips.

Clarinet Basics (pupil's book) ISBN 0-571-51814-1
Clarinet Basics (teacher's book) ISBN 0-571-51815-X
Clarinet Basics (accompaniment CD) ISBN 0-571-52167-3

Clarinet volumes from Faber Music

Howard Blake
'Walking in the Air' from *The Snowman*
ISBN 0-571-58019-X

John Davies & Paul Harris
Second Book of Clarinet Solos
ISBN 0-571-51093-0
80 Graded Studies for Clarinet
Book 1: ISBN 0-571-50951-7   Book 2: ISBN 0-571-50952-5
The *Really* Easy Clarinet Book
ISBN 0-571-51034-5

Paul Harris & Christopher Gunning
Going Solo
ISBN 0-571-51493-6

Paul Harris
Clarinet Carol Time
ISBN 0-571-51183-X
Improve your scales!
Grades 1–3: ISBN 0-571-51475-8   Grades 4–5: ISBN 0-571-51476-6
Improve your sight-reading!
Grades 1–3: ISBN 0-571-51464-2   Grades 4–5: ISBN 0-571-51465-0
Grade 6: ISBN 0-571-51787-0   Grades 7–8: ISBN 0-571-51788-9
Clarinet Basics
Teacher's book: ISBN 0-571-51815-X   Pupil's book: ISBN 0-571-51814-1

Andrew Lloyd Webber
'Memory' from *Cats*
Easy clarinet & piano: ISBN 0-571-51304-2

James Rae
Progressive Jazz Studies
Book 1: ISBN 0-571-51359-X   Book 2: ISBN 0-571-51657-2

Pam Wedgwood
Up-Grade!
Grades 1–2: ISBN 0-571-51819-2   Grades 2–3: ISBN 0-571-51838-9
Christmas Jazzin' About
ISBN 0-571-51585-1
Jazzin' About
ISBN 0-571-51273-9

FABER *ff* MUSIC

fabermusic.com